GRADUATION

INSPIRATION

3

AVONSIDE
PRESS

GRADUATION

INSPIRATION

3

*Yet More Inspiring Quotes
from the World's
Most Uplifting Graduation Speeches:*

*How to Escape the Hamster Wheel
and Live the Life You Want*

EDITED BY
ALISON WILSON

Avonside Press Pty Ltd
PO Box 174, Freshwater Beach, NSW 2096
Australia

*A moment's insight
is sometimes worth
a lifetime's experience*

Oliver Wendell Holmes Jr

Other Books by Alison Wilson

Graduation Inspiration 1

Graduation Inspiration 2

Hold The Phone:
*The Definitive Guide to How to Protect Your
Health from Phones and Wireless*

Hold The Phone: Here's Why:
*Advice from the Experts on How
Phones and Wireless Affect Health*

Websites:

www.holdthephone.co

www.graduationinspiration.com

Contents

Intro

Life is changing so fast that many of us have a hard time trying to keep up, let alone being a step ahead.

As Sheryl Sandberg points out:

"You are entering a different business world than I entered. . . traditional structures are breaking down".

Previous generations were limited by fixed expectations of how their lives 'should' be led; what 'achievement' and 'success' looked like.

Luckily for us the definition of 'success' is much more fluid nowadays, and the ways of achieving the many variations are countless.

Change for some is unsettling, but it presents us with tremendous opportunities. However, to make the most of them we need to evolve and find a way of breaking new ground.

Everyone needs a little inspiration sometimes, and the words within this book (and the previous two) are here to help you look at life a little differently; a little more broadly.

The speakers quoted here have been generous enough to let you have the inside track on how differently they look at life; the insights that allowed them to have rewarding careers, fulfilling relationships and lives of interest; and how jumping out of the box helped them to achieve success on their own terms.

Most of these people are free-thinkers who've made a point of avoiding the mainstream and have soared – not despite that, but because of that.

They'll show how you too can turn your back on the rat race, and lead a life less ordinary.

"We do not need magic to change the world. We carry all the power we need inside ourselves already. We have the power to imagine better."

J K Rowling

What They've Got To Say:

The Quotes

Overcoming Fear

OVERCOMING FEAR

A key component of wisdom is fearlessness - which is not the absence of fear, but rather not letting our fears get in the way.

Arianna Huffington
Sarah Lawrence College 2011

Work on being comfortable in your own skin, but put yourself in uncomfortable spots from time to time. Reach too far.

Learn from your failures.

As Eleanor Roosevelt said, "Anyone can conquer fear by doing the things he fears to do."

Bill Whitaker
Hobart & William Smith Colleges 2008

5

You're going to be doing things and you are going to be scared.

It's natural. Everybody is.

And when that happens, and it's going to happen more than once, do me a favor:

Go back to the days of your childhood. Go in the 100 Acre Wood (*Winnie the Pooh*), take a deep breath and just say:

"I'm stronger than I seem,
I'm braver than I believe,
and I'm smarter than I think."

And then go do it.

James Carville
Hobart & William Smith Colleges 2013

Simply asking ourselves what we want is easy.

Another far more powerful question that can be much harder to explore, but has the potential to bring you breathtaking clarity, is simply: "What do I fear?"

Ed Helms
Knox College 2013

For many of you, the biggest obstacle to getting there will be a fear that you have carried with your since childhood.

The fear of humiliation, of embarrassment, of ridicule.

Jerry Zucker
University of Wisconsin-Madison 2003

That's the amazing thing about failure. It's part success. It's an essential ingredient.

Because you gain courage, and LOSE fear when you *know* - based on your own experience - that you can fail, but you can *recover*.

Savannah Guthrie
Hobart & William Smith Colleges 2012

Life is full of second chances. Remember that. Sometimes even third and fourth chances.

Occasionally even fifth and sixth chances - if you make enough money to afford a good lawyer!

Steve Kroft
Syracuse University 1996

Overcoming Fear

I learned something enduring, in a very short period of time, about life.

And that was that it was glorious and that you had no business taking it for granted. . .

I was never again going to be able to see life as anything except a great gift.

One Thanksgiving I wrote a column about this. . . I was afraid of speaking of plenty in the midst of want. I was afraid of being off the beaten path of anomie and disaffection. But I wrote it anyhow, because I felt it.

And the mail that followed was amazing. Because what people said, again and again, was: "I almost forgot. I almost forgot it was true."

Anna Quindlen
Barnard College 1997

Don't be afraid of trying - of dreaming.
Don't be afraid of failure, or tears.

We all stumble, we all face fear. That's what makes us *human*. But none of us should ever regret.

None of us should ever sit at a grandchild's graduation and think: "I wish that were me starting out all over again. There's so much I'd do differently."

George Bush
Williams College 1996

If you are scared, look into your partner's eyes.

You will feel better.

Amy Poehler
Harvard 2011

Overcoming Fear

People talk about the dangers of rose-colored glasses - but let me tell you, the lenses of self-doubt are far worse.

Jennifer Lee
University of New Hampshire 2014

There are few things more liberating in this life than having your worst fear realized.

Conan O'Brien
Dartmouth College 2011

Take your risks now.

As you grow older, you become more fearful and less flexible.

Amy Poehler
Harvard 2011

I'm here to tell you today that "Fear is good."

To understand why fear is good, one has to stop viewing fear as a feeling, emotion or behavioral command - and start looking at it simply as *information*.

Fear is good because it is our brain's way of identifying the things about which we are ignorant.

Knowing this, we should look at our fear - not as a reason to avoid the things that frighten us - but as a reason to engage them.

Ed Helms
Knox College 2013

Reframing
'Success' and 'Failure'

I feel like success is a spiral with trying, failing, learning and growing; and that's what excellence is also.

You know we never achieve excellence, we always fail. But the process of failing and learning, and growing, and coming closer and closer - to me that's excellence. That's success.

Ben Cohen
Hampshire College 1990

Don't confine yourself to the fair weather races; the easy races, the races you know you can win.

Get out in gale force winds. Know you will capsize - again and again and again and again.

Anne Fadiman
College of the Holy Cross 2013

14

I have always made work that I believe in - not work that *others* felt I should believe in. This is important, because there will be failures.

Your films or books or ideas may get rejected. You will learn to tolerate frustration - take it from me who has had many more failures than successes.

You will knock on doors, some will slam in your face, and you must pick yourself up and knock again for what you believe in. Because many years from now - if you believe in what you have made - it won't matter much whether it was a success or a failure.

There is little joy in a success that you do not believe in. But the joy of having a success that you believe in is immeasurable.

Jehane Noujaim
Northwestern University, Qatar 2014

Like many of you I've had my share of life's personal challenges and failures.

But after many miles on my journey I recognize that each of these difficult periods of life passes, and with each we exit stronger and wiser.

The old saying "This too, shall pass" has certainly proven true for me.

Tim Cook
Auburn University 2010

You will fail at some point in your life. Accept it. You will lose. You will embarrass yourself. You will suck at something. There is no doubt about it . . . I'm telling you, embrace it - because it's inevitable.

Denzel Washington
University of Pennsylvania 2011

16

The biggest surprise of the meeting was . . . that (we) had both learned the same central thing about success. And what we had learned had nothing to do with fame or money or happiness.

It had to do with fear.

Both of us had learned that on occasion, life will look you in the eye and say "Get into the wheelbarrow."

At that moment, all of your knowledge won't matter.

All that will matter is how badly you need to get to the other side of the tightrope - and how much you are afraid of falling.

Marc S Lewis
University of Texas at Austin 2000

And sometimes the things I did really didn't work. But I learned as much from them as I did from the things that worked.

Neil Gaiman
University of the Arts 2012

So you will take risks, and you will have failures. But it's what happens afterwards that is defining.

A failure often does not have to be a failure at all. However, you have to be ready for it: Will you admit when things go wrong? Will you take steps to set them right?

Because the difference between triumph and defeat, you'll find, isn't about willingness to take risks. It's about mastery of rescue.

Atul Gawande
Williams College 2012

18

When things go wrong, there seem to be three main pitfalls to avoid. Three ways to "Fail to Rescue".

You could choose a wrong plan, an inadequate plan, or no plan at all . . .

But recognizing that your expectations are proving wrong - accepting that you need a new plan - is commonly the hardest thing to do.

We have this problem called confidence. To take a risk, you must have confidence in yourself.

Yet you cannot blind yourself to failure, either. Indeed, you must prepare for it.

For, strangely enough, only then is success possible.

Atul Gawande
Williams College 2012

19

I was one of the lucky ones. I graduated with no employable skills (unless you count jury duty).

It meant I had to start from scratch and figure out where I fit in. I didn't have money, but I could afford to fail. And there were many failures.

But I found out what I was good at. I found something I loved.

Jerry Zucker
University of Wisconsin-Madison 2003

Certainty is a moving target. Our first few steps won't be perfect. They never are; but missteps are not missed steps at all. They are opportunities for learning a new perspective.

Omid Kordestani
San Jose State University 2007

There's nothing wrong with failing because you're not good enough. There's nothing sadder than: I could have had it if I'd just tried a little harder.

Jay Leno
Emerson College 2014

The happiest and most successful people I know don't just love what they do, they're obsessed with solving an important problem - something that matters to them.

Drew Houston
Massachusetts Institute of Technology 2013

Sometimes the best way to discover your true calling is by doing something that you're not cut out for.

Katie Couric
Trinity College 2014

It's a mistake to think that numbers or letters in themselves are measures of success. They describe certain forms of achievement, that's all.

It's ridiculous to think that a $90,000-a-year* investment banker is more successful than an elementary school teacher who makes just enough to live on.

(* Salaries have risen somewhat since 1990!)

Cathleen Black
Simmons College 1990

The biggest problem of success is that the world conspires to stop you doing the thing that you do, *because* you are successful.

Neil Gaiman
University of the Arts 2012

22

Thinking BIG, means conjuring up a vision for yourself.

It means taking time, being reflective, and daring to visualize what it would look like if you could wave a magic wand and be exactly where you wanted to be in five years - even if it seems a little unrealistic at the moment.

Savannah Guthrie
Hobart & William Smith Colleges 2012

College is something you complete. Life is something you experience. So don't worry about your grade, or the results or success.

Success is defined in myriad ways, and you will find it. And people will no longer be grading you, but it will come from your own internal sense of decency.

Jon Stewart
The College of William & Mary 2004

Everything I'm truly proud of in this life has been a terrifying prospect to me.

From my first play, to hosting "Saturday Night Live," getting married, being a father, speaking to you today. None of it comes easy. People will tell you to do what makes you happy, but all this has been hard work. And I'm not always happy.

I don't think you should just do what makes you happy. Do what makes you *great*. Do what's uncomfortable and scary and hard, but pays off in the long run.

Be willing to fail. Let yourself fail. Fail in the way and place where you would be proud to fail. Fail and pick yourself up and fail again.

Without that struggle, what is your success anyway?

Charlie Day
Merrimack College 2014

24

You are the lucky few. All of you have been faced with the extra cookie. All of you will be faced with many more of them.

In time you will find it easy to assume that you deserve the extra cookie. For all I know, you may.

But you'll be happier - and the world will be better off - if you at least *pretend* that you don't.

Michael Lewis
Princeton University 2012

There is only one definition of a champion. Only one.

And the true champion is the one who gets up one more time than they're knocked down.

James Carville
Hobart & William Smith Colleges 2013

25

Your path at 22 will not necessarily be your path at 32 or 42. One's dream is constantly evolving, rising and falling, changing course. . . . At the age of 47, after 25 years of obsessively pursuing my dream, that dream changed.

For decades, in show business, the ultimate goal of every comedian was to host The Tonight Show. It was the Holy Grail and, like many people, I thought that achieving that goal would define me as successful.

But that is not true. No specific job or career goal defines me and it should not define you . . .

I am here to tell you that whatever you think your dream is now, it will probably change.

Conan O'Brien
Dartmouth College 2011

Don't be afraid. All you have to know is *who you are* because there is no such thing as failure. There is no such thing as failure.

What other people label or might try to call failure, I have learned is just God's way of pointing you in a new direction.

Oprah Winfrey
Howard University 2007

It is important to have determination, and optimism and patience. If you lack patience, even when you face some small obstacle, you lose courage.

There is a Tibetan saying: "Even if you have failed at something nine times, you have still given it effort nine times."

I think that's important.

Dalai Lama
Emory University 1998

27

Raise the bar higher. OK? It is noisy out there and for some reason, people want to see you fail. But that's not your problem. That is their problem.

I only remember the moments where I tried beyond what I thought I could do. And I do not remember the failures because I didn't.

Sandra Bullock
Warren Easton Charter School 2014

Success will depend on what you do when you fail, because you will fail along the way. We all do.

Rahm Emanuel
George Washington University 2009

Some of the most devastating things that happen to you will teach you the most.

Ellen Degeneres
Tulane University 2009

28

Famous 'Failures'

Because, even those who are famous and successful today once 'failed' – some more than once!

I remember one of the low points in my life, when my second book was rejected by 37 publishers . . .

And then I got an acceptance . . .

So, very often, the difference between success and failure is perseverance.

It's how long can we keep going until success happens. It's getting up one more time than we fall down.

Arianna Huffington
Sarah Lawrence College 2011

29

Famous 'Failures'

A man who worked on cartoons at my company for a while had earlier run a small film studio in Kansas City. He was such an enthusiastic novice that he went broke.

Penniless, he came to the West Coast and created a successful cartoon character. It was stolen from him.

After two such failures, many people would have given up. Instead he tried again . . . and created a cartoon character that became enormously successful.

The character was Mickey Mouse. The cartoonist was Walt Disney. Today I am grateful to both of them for my job.

Michael Eisner
Denison University 1989

Famous 'Failures'

You must have a high threshold for frustration.

Take it from the guy who was turned down by every studio in Hollywood.

You must knock on doors until your knuckles bleed. Doors will slam in your face, I guarantee it.

You must pick yourself up, dust yourself off, and go back and knock again.

It's the only way to achieve your goals in life.

Michael Uslan
Indiana University 2006

31

Famous 'Failures'

I've made some bad decisions.

I lost a decade of my life to cocaine addiction.

You know how I got addicted to cocaine? I tried it. The problem with drugs is that they work, right up until the moment that they decimate your life.

Try cocaine, and you'll become addicted to it. Become addicted to cocaine, and you will either be dead, or you will wish you were dead.

But it will only be one or the other.

My big fear was that I wasn't going to be able to write without it . . .

Last month I celebrated my 11-year anniversary of not using coke.

In that 11 years, I've written three television series, three movies, a Broadway play, won the Academy Award and taught my daughter all the lyrics to "Pirates of Penzance".

Aaron Sorkin
Syracuse University 2012

Surviving Challenges

Surviving Challenges

So, you start out in the dark. You don't know where you're going . . .

Of course, you will run into danger, because no one else has ever taken this particular journey before.

But all the stories tell us what where we stumble, there we may find treasure.

Lee Smith
Hollins College 1993

Wherever you think you're heading right now might turn out to take a completely different route down a entirely different path . . .

And what looks like an ending might actually be the start of a brand new beginning.

Annie Lennox
Berkelee College of Music 2013

It's important not to retreat in the face of setbacks.

Don't take yourself too seriously . . .

One of the most underestimated tools in politics, in leadership, in life, is a sense of humor. The ability to laugh not just at others, but at ourselves.

Dan Glickman
Hobart & William Smith Colleges 2010

When you start out you have to deal with the problems of failure.

You need to be thick-skinned - to learn that not every project will survive.

Neil Gaiman
University of the Arts 2012

36

Surviving Challenges

If I could do so much of my life over . . . I'd have taken in the beauty of the moment, and greeted everything in my life with a big "Yes, and . . ."

Whatever it is, the good, the bad, the thrilling, the heartbreaking, every emotion, occurrence, event, person, place or thing - you will experience them all.

That's the "Yes" I'm talking about.

And the acceptance and embrace of it, with all your heart, and doing something with it - that's the "and."

You accept influence. And then you exert influence.

Jane Lynch
Smith College 2012

Whatever you resist persists.

My friend Eckhart Tolle puts it like this: He says, "Don't react against a bad situation. *Merge* with that situation instead, and the solution will arise from the challenge."

Because surrendering yourself doesn't mean giving up; it means acting with responsibility.

Oprah Winfrey
Stanford 2008

How you live matters.

You're going to fall down but the world doesn't care how many times you fall down. As long as it's one fewer than the number of times you get back up.

Aaron Sorkin
Syracuse University 2012

When you gain or lose material things, remember how silly they really are.

How little they mean relative to your health and relationships.

Salman Khan
MIT University 2012

The road less travelled is sometimes fraught with barricades, bumps, and uncharted terrain.

But it is on that road where your character is truly tested - and your personal growth realized.

Katie Couric
Williams College 2007

Changing the world can happen anywhere, and anyone can do it . . .

It matters not your gender, your ethnic or religious background, your orientation, or your social status.

Our struggles in this world are similar and the lessons to overcome those struggles and to move forward - changing ourselves and the world around us - will apply equally to all.

William McRaven
University of Texas 2014

Hope is a renewable option.

If you run out of it at the end of the day, you get to start over in the morning.

Barbara Kingsolver
DePauw University 1994

Surviving Challenges

The best advice I can give anybody about going out into the world is this: "Don't do it."

I have been out there. It is a mess.

Russel Baker
Connecticut College 1995

Just keep trying! Never give up. Never, never give up! Because the only person that can stop you is. . . you!

Yvonne Thornton
Tuskegee University 2003

Never be discouraged. Never hold back. Give everything you've got.

Denzel Washington
University of Pennsylvania 2011

Some of you may think that these troubled times are beyond help. Some may think it's everyone for themselves. Our goals and dreams are just fantasies, drifting on the wind.

Well you would be wrong . . .

You live in a world not filled with unsolvable obstacles but in a world where the possibilities are greater than ever in history.

Whether or not you think you can, you are right.

A young president Kennedy once said. "If not us who? If not now when?"

Now is your when.

W Douglas Smith
DeVry University 2010

BEING HUMAN(E)

In a world that seems increasingly snarky and judgmental, be kind.

Be kind to your friends.
Be kind to your family.
Be kind to yourselves.

And remember, just as you are, everyone really is just doing the best they can.

Katie Couric
Williams College 2007

Develop and protect a moral sensibility and demonstrate the character to apply it.

Dream big. Work hard. Think for yourself.

Love everything you love, everyone you love, with all your might.

David McCullough Jr
Wellesley High School 2012

Motivation comes from working on things we care about but it also comes from working with people we care about. And in order to care about someone, you have to know them.

You have to know what they love and hate, what they feel, not just what they think.

If you want to win hearts and minds, you have to lead with your heart as well as your mind.

Sheryl Sandberg
Harvard Business School 2012

If you truly care for people you won't judge them. And then you will learn to appreciate the uniqueness in every single soul.

Dolly Parton
University of Tennessee 2009

But there will also be moments when you have a different point of view, because you're wrong . . .

Because you're 23, and you should shut up and listen to somebody who's been around the block . . .

I will always cringe remembering those little embarrassing moments when I said something dumb on a conference call.

When my inexperience poked through; when I should have been more solicitous of the judgment of those around me.

There's a reminder that it's not mutually exclusive to be confident and humble; to be sceptical and eager to learn.

Jon Lovett
Pitzer 2013

Being Human(e)

If you find yourself, in your life, in an argument with someone whom you respect, whom you care deeply about – It's not an easy thing to do - but try to surrender your ego to the shared identity of the relationship that you have with that person.

If possible, do exactly the opposite of what your pride and ego tell you in the heat of battle.

And if you have the strength to do it - right when you're about to get in that last word, and you're about to say that kind of maybe vindictive or below the belt thing - just pause.

Don't do anything, and try to just give them a super-mega hug.

Salman Khan
MIT University 2012

Be compassionate to everyone.

Don't just search for whatever it is that annoys and frightens you. See beyond those things to the basic human being. Especially see the child in the man or woman.

Even if they are destroying you, allow a moment to see how lost in their own delusion and suffering they are.

Alice Walker
Naropa University 2007

Teamwork is everything . . .

The person who works the hardest and works with others the best, who says "We" and "Us", not "I" and "Me" - is the person who wins.

Michael Bloomberg
University of North Carolina 2012

Ultimately, it turns out, we all have an intrinsic need to pursue purposes larger than ourselves; purposes worth making sacrifices for.

People often say: find your passion. But there's more to it than that. Not all passions are enough.

Just existing for your desires feels empty and insufficient, because our desires are fleeting and insatiable.

You need a loyalty.

The only way life is not meaningless is to see yourself as part of something greater: a family, a community, a society.

Atul Gawande
University of North Carolina 2014

Being Human(e)

When someone who cares about you hugs you, hug them back with two arms.

Don't do the one-arm hug, because when you hug with two arms, it allows you to lean on somebody - and we always need someone to lean on.

Sandra Bullock
Warren Easton Charter School 2014

What should you do?
How should you behave?

Well, do things in a group.
Don't do things by yourself.
Groups are stronger; groups are faster.

None of us is as smart as all of us.

Eric Schmidt
Carnegie-Mellon University 2009

And so, a prediction, and my heartfelt wish for you: As you get older, your self will diminish and you will grow in love.

YOU will gradually be replaced by LOVE.

If you have kids that will be a huge moment in your process of self-diminishment. You really won't care what happens to you, as long as they benefit.

George Saunders
Syracuse University 2013

I cannot stress enough that the answer to a lot of your life's questions is often in someone else's face. Try putting your iPhones down every once in a while and look at people's faces. People's faces will tell you amazing things.

Amy Poehler
Harvard 2011

51

Become the best listener you can be.

Learn to listen with the instruments of the body, the feelings of the heart, the logic of the mind and the stillness of your soul.

As you listen deeply, reflect on the following questions:
What am I observing?
What am I feeling?
What is the need of the moment?
What is the best way to fulfil this need?

Deepak Chopra
Hartwick College 2013

Your families brought you here and you brought them here. Please keep them close and remember, they are what really matters in life.

Larry Page
University of Michigan 2009

Wisdom is like frequent-flyer miles and scar tissue:

If it does accumulate, that happens by accident while you're trying to do something else.

Barbara Kingsolver
Duke University 2008

Recognize that material loss or gain will all happen. But when it happens be upset a little bit, or be happy a little bit, but keep it all in perspective.

They're all silly relative to the things that matter: your health and your relationships.

Salman Khan
MIT University 2012

Staying True To You

Even though you will fall down and foul up and make mistakes as I have - as everyone does - you will make this world a better place if you can bring to it your own unique and individual excellence and quality and originality.

This is your gift to give. This is the greatest service you can render to your community, and to others.

Billy Joel
Fairfield University 1991

Eleanor Roosevelt once said that: "Within all of us there are two sides. One reaches for the stars, the other descends to the level of beasts."

That is not only a statement of fact. It is a presentation of choice.

Madeleine Albright
Barnard College 1995

55

Believe and be you. Be unique. Be prepared to be alone sometimes when you're unique. It's not a bad thing. You could travel with the sheep, follow everybody else's stuff - but then you're not you.

Whoopi Goldberg
SCAD Savannah 2011

If you have 50 years left, or 50 days left, or even 50 minutes left, it's never too late to become what you might have been.

John Jacob Scherer
Roanoke College 2010

As best we know we have one life. In it, you must trust your own voice, your own ideas, your honestly and venerability. And though this you will find your way.

Charlie Day
Merrimack College 2014

56

It's our collection of screw-ups and idiosyncrasies and memories and stories and lessons learned that make us weird and interesting.

Weirdness is why we adore our friends.

I can see the weirdness in mutual recognition of weirdness in your eyes as you look around each other.

Weirdness is what bonds us to our colleagues.

Weirdness is what sets us apart, gets hired.

Be your unapologetically weird self. In fact being weird may even find you the ultimate happiness.

Chris Sacca
University of Minnesota 2011

As you start your journey, the first thing you should do is throw away that store-bought map and begin to draw your own.

Michael Dell
University of Texas at Austin 2003

There is nothing more beautiful than finding your course as you believe you bob aimlessly in the current.

And wouldn't you know that your path was there all along, waiting for you to knock, waiting for you to become.

This path does not belong to your parents, your teachers, your leaders, or your lovers.

Your path is your character defining itself more and more every day.

Jodie Foster
University of Pennsylvania 2006

Staying True To You

All of us, and especially leaders, need to speak and hear the truth . . .

Think about how people speak in a typical workforce. Rather than say "I disagree with our expansion strategy" or, better yet, "This seems truly stupid." they say:

"I think there are many good reasons why we're entering this new line of business, and I'm certain the management team has done a thorough ROI analysis, but I'm not sure we fully considered the downstream effects of taking this step forward at this time."

As we would say at Facebook on the internet, three letters: WTF.

Truth is better used by using simple language.

Sheryl Sandberg
Harvard Business School 2012

You are capable of more than you think.

If you've ever smashed a mosquito on your arm, there is a murderous Richard III inside you.

If you've ever caught your breath at the sight of someone dipping their toes into Lake Mendota in the late afternoon sun over at the Union, you, too, have Romeo's fluttering heart.

Bradley Whitford
University of Wisconsin 2004

The most important piece of advice I can give you on the path to happiness is not just to be yourself, but be your weird self.

It takes too much energy to be anything but your weird self.

Chris Sacca
University of Minnesota 2011

Staying True To You

You're too good for schadenfreude.
You're too good for gossip and snark.
You're too good for intolerance . . .

It's worth mentioning that you're too good to think people who disagree with you are your enemy.

Aaron Sorkin
Syracuse University 2012

To live is to choose. But to choose well, you must know:

Who you are.
What you stand for.
Where you want to go, and
Why you want to get there.

Kofi Annan
Massachusetts Institute of Technology 1997

My advice is: Don't follow the advice of others.

I am not suggesting that you ignore advice, but just don't let your advisers make decisions for you.

Robert Kraft
Suffolk University 2013

Sometimes you're going to be inexperienced, naïve, untested and totally right. And then, in those moments you have to make a choice: is this a time to speak up or hold back? And it won't be easy . . .

If you see something, say something. And I've tried to honor that ever since. To call B.S. when I see it, and to not be afraid to get in people's faces.

Jon Lovett
Pitzer 2013

We all pay for our choices, and whatever life we choose determines the kind of payment we make.

There really is a palpable moral component to our beings, and it can be contaminated.

Moral contamination almost never announces itself. It is always a very small, seemingly silent, inconsequential event, but it is like radiation.

It accumulates, and there are no permissible safe levels.

E L Doctorow
Hobart & William Smith Colleges 1979

Hell, is realizing the truth too late.

Dan Quayle
DePauw University 1982

Take the time to think about what you choose to do, to reflect, to be sure you are living with integrity and honesty.

When you are 90 years old, you will want to look back on your life and be able to tell a story you are proud of.

When you are in moments of transition, think about the story you will want to tell your grandkids.

Time is too precious to be wasted doing things you are not proud of.

Jehane Noujaim
Northwestern University, Qatar 2014

Learn to be independent of the good and bad opinion of others.

Deepak Chopra
Hartwick College 2013

64

Staying True To You

Consider what people think of you.

But don't be *afraid* of what they think of you.

Anders Holm
University of Wisconsin-Madison 2013

Whatever it was that got you to this school, don't let it go. Whatever kept you here, don't let that go.

Believe in your friends. Believe that what you and your friends have to say . . . that the way you're saying it – is something new in the world.

And don't stop. Just hold on.
And keep loving what you love . . .

Robert Krulwich
Berkeley Journalism School 2011

I think this may be my favorite truth:

The world needs you.

Now, the world may not exactly realize it, but wow, does it need you. It is yearning, starving, dying for you and your healing offer of service through your art.

We need you to help us understand that which is bigger than ourselves; so that we can stop feeling so small, so isolated, so helpless.

So that, in our fear, we stop contributing that which is unique to us: that distinct, rare, individual quality which the world is desperately crying out for, and eagerly awaiting.

Joyce DiDonato
Juilliard 2014

What you do will matter. Principles will matter. And those of you who stand for something can make a difference - even if at first you stand alone.

Marty Baron
Lehigh University 2014

You have, which is a rare thing, the ability and the responsibility to listen to the dissent in yourself - to at least give it the floor. Because it is the key, not only to consciousness, but to real growth.

Joss Whedon
Wesleyan University 2013

Understand that one day you will have the power to make a difference. So use it well.

Mindy Kaling
Harvard Law School 2014

Sometimes it seems as though many of us will be satisfied with nothing if we do not achieve Utopia.

And we become obsessed by the desire to change the world, and never get around to assuming the almost unbearable responsibility for our own lives.

Julius Lester
Hampshire College 1984

Be fearless.

It is hard to make progress without breaking a little crockery - and don't be afraid to go down fighting, if you're fighting a righteous battle.

Stick to your guns and to your principles.

Susan Rice
Stanford 2010

68

STAYING TRUE TO YOU

I hope you'll always . . . only do things that make you proud.

So that you can truly be your own hero.

Marc S Lewis
University of Texas at Austin 2000

You will find true success and happiness if you have only one goal, there really is only one, and that is this:

To fulfil the highest most truthful expression of yourself as a human being.

You want to max out your humanity by using your energy to lift yourself up, your family and the people around you.

Oprah Winfrey
Harvard 2013

I've learned that it's possible to set your sights high and achieve your dreams and do it with integrity, character, and love.

And each day that you're moving toward your dreams without compromising who you are, you're winning.

Michael Dell
University of Texas at Austin 2003

You count. You make a difference.

You can add to the sum of beauty and joy and love and understanding in the world. Or you can subtract from those already scarce enough commodities.

What you do matters.

Vincent Barnett
Williams College 1975

70

STAYING TRUE TO YOU

According to a survey of 75 business leaders with Stanford MBAs, the most important predictor of success is self-awareness.

That means knowing - and accepting - your own strengths and weaknesses.

In other words: Look at yourself honestly.

Understand your passions, your skills, your temperament - and your limitations.

If you're a square peg, no matter how hard you - and others - try, you're just not going to fit very well into a round hole.

Katie Couric
Williams College 2007

Try and make people laugh. If you can't do that, find space in your life for something that makes you laugh. It's not impossible.

Greet the many challenges that this world is going to offer you with passion and courage and conviction, yes, but also with some degree of levity.

Chris Regan
Ithaca 2014

As highly motivated people, we rush ahead in pursuit of great experiences and great success. Sometimes we run so fast in search of the experiences we want, we miss the very experiences we need.

It is not a waste of time to take your time.

Jehane Noujaim
Northwestern University, Qatar 2014

Remember, *how* you get things done is just as important as getting them done.

Your integrity is one of the most valuable possessions you have.

Protect it. Cultivate it. Wear it with pride.

Mary Barra
University of Michigan 2014

The greatest creative challenge is the struggle to be the architect of your own life.

So be patient. Do not compromise.

And give your destiny time to find you.

Wade Davis
Colorado College 2010

There will be many, many times in the course of your professional and personal lives where you will be encouraged - in shockingly plain ways - to take the easy way, to go along with the group in contradiction to your own principles . . .

Standing up for one's own integrity makes you no friends. It is costly.

Yet defiance of the mob, in the service of that which is right, is one of the highest expressions of courage I know.

Gabrielle Giffords
Scripps College 2009

You don't need to change yourself. Ever. You need to come home to yourself. And that changes everything.

John Jacob Scherer
Roanoke College 2010

Trust, Intuition, and Being Present

Be present. I would encourage you with all my heart - just to be present.

Be present and open to the moment that is unfolding before you.

Because, ultimately, your life is made up of moments. So don't miss them by being lost in the past, or anticipating the future.

Jessica Lange
Sarah Lawrence College 2008

Be open to opportunities when they occur.

Embrace them. Enjoy them. And overcome them.

They are the experiences that will make you unique; the milestones that define your life.

Mary Barra
University of Michigan 2014

Develop your own compass and trust it. Take risks. Dare to fail.

Aaron Sorkin
Syracuse University 2012

If you ever feel inspired, take action with it. Don't let anyone tell you why you shouldn't. At least lace up and give it a try.

Salman Khan
MIT University 2012

Life is an improvisation. You have no idea what's going to happen next and you are mostly just making things up as you go along.

And, like improv, you cannot 'win' your life. Even when it might look like you're winning.

Stephen Colbert
Northwestern University 2011

77

You can't plan a script. The beauty of improvisation is that you're experiencing it in the moment.

If you try to plan what the next line is supposed to be, you're just going to be disappointed when the other people on stage with you don't do, or say, what you want them to do. And you'll stand there, frozen.

Be in this moment. Be here in this moment. Now be here, in *this* moment.

Dick Costolo
University of Michigan 2013

A simple principle for the most important decisions in your life: Trust your intuition. And then work with everything you have.

Tim Cook
Auburn University 2010

Conspirators are the ones that show up. They just show up.

And what do I mean by that? I mean that we go *through* life all the time, but we don't always show up.

We may be there in body but we're not there in spirit.

And we begin to erode the truth of who we are. We fail to live our authenticity.

A great president, Lincoln, said that:

"Everyone is born an original but, sadly, most die copies"

Because they don't show up.

Cory Booker
Stanford 2012

Each step forward in technological communication has made things more convenient.

But each step has also made it easier, just a little bit easier, to avoid the emotional work of being present.

To write 'LOL' rather than to actually laugh out loud;

To send a crying emoji rather than actually crying;

To convey information rather than humanity.

It's never been easier to say nothing.

Jonathan Safran Foer
Middlebury College 2013

Too often people think about intuition as the same as relying on luck or faith. At least as I see it, nothing could be further from the truth.

Intuition can tell you that of the doors that are open to you, which one you should walk through.

But intuition cannot prepare you for what's on the other side of that door.

Tim Cook
Auburn University 2010

To people in the modern world, true silence is something we rarely experience. It is almost as if we conspire to avoid it.

Silence is disturbing. It is disturbing because it is the wavelength of the soul.

Sting
Berklee College of Music 1994

81

The work will never end.

This may sound dreadfully daunting . . . But what I have found is that when things become overwhelming – which they will, repeatedly - whether it's via unexpected, rapid success or as heart-wrenching, devastating failure - the way back to your centre is simply to *return to the work*.

Often times it will be the only thing that makes sense. And it is there where you will find solace and truth.

All it asks is that you show up, fully present as you did when you first discovered the magic of your own artistic world when you were young.

Bring that innocent, childlike sense of wonder to your craft, and do whatever you need to find that truth again.

It will continually teach you how to be present, how to be alive, and how to let go.

Therein lies not only your artistic freedom, but your personal freedom as well!

Joyce DiNato
Juillard 2014

Doubt means don't.
This is what I've learned.

There are many times when you don't know what to do.

When you don't know what to do, get still, get very still - until you *do* know what to do.

Oprah Winfrey
Stanford 2008

If I could do so much of my life over, I would have taken more moments like this to *breathe*.

I would have spent more time focusing on what was right in front of me, instead of recoiling from what is, because it didn't look or feel exactly as I imagined it.

I wouldn't have been forever trying to look around the corner to see "What's next, what's next?!"

I'd have taken in the beauty of the moment, and greeted everything in my life with a big "Yes!"

Jane Lynch
Smith College 2012

When Clay (Christensen) graduated from college he decided that his most important and immediate task was to find a purpose for his life.

He was enrolled in a program in Oxford but he took off an hour each day to study, to pray and to think about his purpose.

The program he was in was very demanding but each evening, no matter what, he took off an hour to find his purpose.

He calls that enterprise the single most useful thing he's ever done.

David Brooks
Rice University 2011

The Road
Less Travelled

The Road Less Travelled

There is no straight path from your seat today to where you are going.

Don't try to draw that line.

You will not just get it wrong, you'll miss big opportunities . . .

Careers are not ladders, those days are long gone, but jungle gyms. Don't just move up and down; don't just look up - look backwards, sideways around corners.

Your career and your life will have starts and stops, and zigs and zags.

Don't stress out about the white space - the path you can't draw - because therein lies both the surprises and the opportunities.

Sheryl Sandberg
Harvard 2014

There are CEO's that really do think for themselves and are innovative. They go against the trend.

That is what you should seek to be when you go out into the world.

You should try to stand up against the trend.

Carl Icahn
Drexel University 2008

What we need are men and women who will dare to break the mould of tired thinking . . .

Who just won't buy somebody's saying: "We've always done it this way. This way is good enough."

William Zinsser
Wesleyan University 1988

88

What's your big idea?

What are you willing to spend your moral capital, your intellectual capital, your cash, your sweat equity in pursuing . . .

The world is more malleable than you think, and it's waiting for you to hammer it into shape.

Bono
University of Pennsylvania 2004

A lot of the time the experts, the people who are supposed to be able to tell you what to do, will tell you that you can't do something. Even when you know you can.

And a lot of the time it's your friends . . . who tell you you *can* do it.

Mark Zuckerberg
Belle Haven Elementary School 2011

People who know what they are doing know the rules, and know what is possible, and what is impossible.

You do not. And you should not.

The rules on what is possible and impossible in the arts were made by people who had not tested the bounds of the possible by going beyond them.

And you can.

If you don't know it's impossible, it's easier to do.

And because nobody's done it before, they haven't made up rules to stop anyone from doing that particular thing again.

Neil Gaiman
University of the Arts 2012

The really important kind of freedom involves attention, and awareness, and discipline, and effort.

And being able truly to care about other people and to sacrifice for them, over and over, in myriad petty little unsexy ways, every day. That is real freedom.

The alternative is unconsciousness, the default-setting, the "rat race". The constant gnawing sense of having had and lost some infinite thing.

David Foster Wallace
Kenyon College 2005

I would urge you to be as impudent as you dare. Be bold, be bold, be bold!

Susan Sontag
Wellesley College 1983

If, on the other hand, you do what's expected of you, or what you're *supposed* to do, and things go poorly, or chaos ensues, as it surely will – you will look to external sources for what to do next. Because that will be the habit you've created for yourself.

You'll be standing there, frozen on the stage of your own life.

If you're just filling a role, you will be blindsided.

Dick Costolo
University of Michigan 2013

The fulfilled life is a consequence, a gratifying by-product. It's what happens when you're thinking about more important things.

David McCullough Jr
Wellesley High School 2012

No matter what your field, you are blessed if you attain success by working your way up the ladder, one rung at a time.

So don't feel bad if it takes you longer than you thought it would, you'll know more than the other guys when you do get to the top.

Denise Di Novi
Simmons College 1997

When you get too comfortable, move on.

You should always try to find the toughest audience you can.

It's how you get better at what you do.

Jay Leno
Emerson College 2014

93

As you go about changing the world, continuously challenge yourselves. Get out of your comfort zone. Go travel the world we share. Learn more languages.

Get grit in your eyes, and sand in your hair, and service in your soul.

Susan Rice
Stanford 2010

Dream bigger - both for yourself and the world around you.

Your life's course will not be determined by doing the things that you are certain you can do. Those are the easy things.

It will be determined by whether you try the things that are hard.

Sheryl Sandberg
City Colleges of Chicago 2014

The Road Less Travelled

To make it in any profession and any job you have to work hard and find a way to love it.

All forms of success, from being a great mother to being a great actor, take tenacity and determination.

They say for every light on Broadway there is a broken heart, an unrealized dream.

And that's the same in every profession.

So you have to want it more than anyone else. And you have to be your own champion.

Be your own superstar.
Blaze your own path.

Sutton Foster
Ball State University 2012

Try never to be the smartest person in the room.

And if you are, I suggest you invite smarter people . . . or find a different room.

In professional circles it's called networking. In organizations it's called team building. And in life it's called family, friends, and community.

Michael Dell
University of Texas at Austin 2003

I think it is often easier to make progress on mega ambitious dreams.

I know that sounds completely nuts - but since no one else is crazy enough to do it, you have little competition.

Larry Page
University of Michigan 2009

Think of the world as a big glass of water with some salt in it.

You have a choice.

You can try to pick out all the salt, or you can keep pouring in more water so eventually it gets less bitter.

As you begin your new journey, you can try to remove everything that you find distasteful in the world. Or you can just pour in more love.

It's the only thing that the more you give away, the more you have.

Jerry Zucker
University of Wisconsin-Madison 2003

THE ROAD LESS TRAVELLED

If every one of you changed the lives of just ten people - and each one of those folks changed the lives of another ten people, just ten - then in five generations,125 years - the class of 2014 will have changed the lives of 800 million people.

800 million people - think of it - over twice the population of the United States.

Go one more generation and you can change the entire population of the world - 8 billion people.

If you think it's hard to change the lives of ten people - change their lives forever - you're wrong.

I saw it happen every day in Iraq and Afghanistan.

William McRaven
University of Texas 2014

98

Silence in the face of injustice and wrongdoing encourages that injustice, and fuels that wrongdoing.

If you don't speak out, who will?

Elizabeth Holtzman
Simmons College 1981

There's even a higher and more rare level of happiness. It goes by many names: excellence, meaning and fulfilment.

It involves doing many things that are painful not pleasurable; involves doing things that sometimes costs you your friends - and it involves achieving some large thing for the world.

David Brooks
Rice University 2011

Take action. Every story you've ever connected with, every leader you've ever admired, every puny little thing that you've ever accomplished is the result of taking action.

You have a choice. You can either be a passive victim of circumstance or you can be the active hero of your own life.

Action is the antidote to apathy and cynicism and despair.

Bradley Whitford
University of Wisconsin 2004

Don't think you've got your career all figured out. No plan for the rest of your life ever works out the way you thought it would.

Michael Bloomberg
University of North Carolina 2012

'Learning how to think' really means learning how to exercise some control over how and what you think.

It means being conscious and aware enough to choose what you pay attention to. And to choose how you construct meaning from experience.

David Foster Wallace
Kenyon College 2005

Biological evolution has been summed up in the phrase of "survival of the fittest".

But with overpopulation and over-consumption of resources, the future belongs to "survival of the wisest."

Deepak Chopra
Hartwick College 2013

I'm very grateful for my life, but if I had but one wish for you, it would be for you to dream more . . .

Do not confuse dreams with wishes. There is a difference.

Dreams are where you visualize yourself being successful at what's important to you to accomplish.

Dreams build convictions, because you work hard to pay the price to make sure that they come true.

Wishes are hoping good things will happen to you.

But there is no fire in your gut that causes you to put everything forth to overcome all the obstacles.

Dolly Parton
University of Tennessee 2009

Dare to believe that one person really can make a difference. Dare to dream. Dare to fail. Dare to make a few mistakes along the way.

And most of all, dare to reach out your hand into the darkness, to pull another hand into the light. Because when you do, you'll find that it's your own hand.

Norman B Rice
Whitman College 1998

You can be as earnest and ridiculous as you need to be, if you don't attempt it in isolation.

The ridiculously earnest are known to travel in groups. And they are known to change the world. Look at you. That could be you.

Barbara Kingsolver
Duke University 2008

103

Please don't wait for leaders on a white horse to save us. Instead, turn to the leader in the mirror.

Tap into your own leadership potential because the world desperately needs you.

And that means daring to take risks and to fail, as many times as it takes, along the way to success - and more important, to re-making the world and to do it all with more balance, more joy, more sleep, and more gratitude.

Arianna Huffington
Sarah Lawrence College 2011

I learned to write by writing. I tended to do anything as long as it felt like an adventure, and to stop when it felt like work. Which meant that life did not feel like work.

Neil Gaiman
University of the Arts 2012

Changing the world doesn't happen all at once. It isn't a big bang.

It's an evolution; the sum of a billion tiny sparks.

And some of those sparks will have to come from you.

Katie Couric
American University 2014

Don't know that you can't fly, and you can soar like an eagle.

Don't end up regretting what you did not do because you were too lazy, or too frightened to soar.

Soar to the Heavens. You can do it.

Earl Baaken
University of Hawaii 2004

No matter how scared you are; how intimidating the job market is; how worrisome the economy; how insecure you feel deep down about whether you really have what it takes . . .

You don't have to settle.

Your job right now is to dream big, extravagant, borderline unrealistic dreams.

Savannah Guthrie
Hobart & William Smith Colleges 2012

A LIFE OF

HEART & PASSION

Find your passion and follow it.

If there is anything I have learned in my life you will not find that passion in things, and you will not find that passion in money.

Because the more things and the more money you have, the more you will just look around and use that as the metric. And there will always be someone with more.

Randy Pausch
Carnegie-Mellon University 2008

I wish I could tell you the secret to being forever young, but no one's figured that out yet.

But if you see the glass half full, simplify your life, and give yourself to a worthy cause, you will be forever happy.

Bert Jacobs
University of New Hampshire 2010

Elie Weisel once said, "The opposite of love isn't hate, the opposite of love is indifference."

Hold on to the wonderful idealism you have about the world, and your ability to change it, for as long as you can and if possible, for your entire lives. Tune out the cynics who tell you that you can't.

Katie Couric
Williams College 2007

When people ask what makes for success, I think there is only one very simple answer.

You have to do, in your life and with your life, what turns you on. Anything else is a waste of time. If you know where your own button is, press it.

Malcolm Forbes
Syracuse University 1988

109

I went to college thinking I had it all figured out and I knew exactly what I wanted to be - a doctor.

But when I took the first pre-med requirement, chemistry, I fell flat on my face.

I then began taking photography classes and realized that I had found my passion.

My mother was the one who finally said:

"You have to follow your heart, because if you are not happy, you are not going to succeed."

Jehane Noujaim
Northwestern University, Qatar 2014

A LIFE OF HEART & PASSION

How will you use your gifts? What choices will you make?

Will inertia be your guide, or will you follow your passions?

Will you follow dogma, or will you be original?

Will you choose a life of ease, or a life of service and adventure?

Will you wilt under criticism, or will you follow your convictions?

Will you bluff it out when you're wrong, or will you apologize?

Will you guard your heart against rejection, or will you act when you fall in love?

Will you play it safe, or will you be a little bit swashbuckling?

When it's tough, will you give up, or will you be relentless?

Will you be a cynic, or will you be a builder?

Will you be clever at the expense of others, or will you be kind?

Jeff Bezos
Princeton 2010

Pursuing your dream. I believe that is the path you should follow.

That is why you *have* the dream - to be on the road that you should be on.

If you follow that road, you might not end up at your dream, but you will end up doing something that gives you immense satisfaction.

Lewis Black
University of California at San Diego 2013

112

Sometimes life hits you in the head with a brick. Don't lose faith.

I'm convinced that the only thing that kept me going was that I loved what I did.

Steve Jobs
Stanford 2005

A central wisdom I learned years ago: The richest and fullest lives attain an inner balance of work, love and play, in equal order. That to pursue one to the disregard of others is to open oneself to ultimate sadness in older age.

Whereas to pursue all three with equal dedication is to make possible an old age filled with serenity, peace and fulfilment.

Doris Kearns Goodwin
Dartmouth College 1998

Do those things that incline you toward the big questions, and avoid the things that would reduce you and make you trivial.

That luminous part of you that exists beyond personality - your soul, if you will - is as bright and shining as any that has ever been. Bright as Shakespeare's, bright as Gandhi's, bright as Mother Theresa's.

Clear away everything that keeps you separate from this secret luminous place. Believe it exists, come to know it better, nurture it, share its fruits tirelessly.

And someday, in 80 years, when you're 100, and I'm 134, and we're both so kind and loving we're nearly unbearable, drop me a line, let me know how your life has been.

I hope you will say: "It has been so wonderful."

George Saunders
Syracuse University 2013

You control your future.
You control your destiny . . .

Choose to create the future you want.
Choose to live lives that *matter*.

Choose to follow that about which you are
passionate.

Patrick Corvington
Hobart & William Smith Colleges 2011

Know what you love.

And even if you can't begin in the work you
love, find what you love in the work you're
doing - and it will be like a star that will
guide you to the next place.

Diane Sawyer
University of Illinois at Champaign-Urbana 1997

I can assure you that awards have very little bearing on my own personal happiness, my own sense of wellbeing and purpose in the world.

That comes from studying the world, feeling the world with empathy in my work.

It comes from staying alert and alive and involved in the lives of the people that I love, and the people in the wider world who need my help.

Meryl Streep
Barnard College 2010

You'll find that curiosity, enthusiasm, and passion are very contagious.

Eric Schmidt
Carnegie-Mellon University 2009

As each of you look toward your future always focus on finding that which you do well, and that which you love doing.

Do something that gives you satisfaction every day and makes our society a better place. Do something that helps your fellow citizens. . . . Money and position will or will not follow, but satisfaction will always be there.

Always have a purpose in life that is beyond position and money.

Coliln Powell
Northeastern University 2012

Define yourself by what you love. We have a tendency to define ourselves in opposition to stuff . . . Be *pro* stuff, not just anti stuff.

Tim Minchin
University of Western Australia 2013

Love your work. If you always put your heart into everything you do, you really can't lose.

Whether you wind up making a lot of money or not, you will have had a wonderful time. And no one will ever be able to take that away from you.

Alan Alda
Connecticut College 1980

Be passionate. Do what you love, even if you don't love it every day . . .

I decided to pursue the profession that made me excited to get up in the morning, and that excitement sustained me through the long hours and the inevitable failures and disappointments. You'll also be good at what gets you going.

Katie Couric
Williams College 2007

Don't overuse the word "love". It's just the way people talk and it's probably harmless, but you shouldn't forget the real thing. The real thing is great.

It's just not so easy with actual human beings, but if you work at it and you get it right, it will make you happier than anything else you do in your life.

Jerry Zucker
University of Wisconsin-Madison 2003

As you're reaching higher, please have some fun along the way - lots of fun.

Promise us that you will travel, that you will work so hard it hurts, love so deeply it hurts, laugh so hard it hurts.

Bill Whitaker
Hobart & William Smith Colleges 2008

119

A LIFE OF HEART & PASSION

The third thing not to worry about is the question: Will I find my passion? Commencement speakers are always telling you to find your passion. This is the biggest load of crap old people have ever foisted on the young.

No, you will not find your passion. *Your passion will find you.* Relax and wait for it.

David Brooks
Sewanee University of the South 2013

When you're doing what you love to do, you become resilient. Because that's the habit you create for yourself. You create a habit of taking chances on yourself, and making bold choices in service to doing what you love.

Dick Costolo
University of Michigan 2013

120

Your calling isn't something that somebody can tell you about. It's what you *feel*.

It's a part of your life force. It is the thing that gives you juice. The thing that you are supposed to do.

And nobody can tell you what that is. You know it inside yourself.

Oprah Winfrey
Howard University 2007

Being happy is more than just something to hope for. It's something to expect.

When you do this, when you tune out the critical voices in your head and embrace what your heart is saying - you don't just make your own life better. You make the world better.

Gabrielle Giffords
Scripps College 2009

You've got to find what you love.

And that is as true for your work as it is for your lovers.

Your work is going to fill a large part of your life - and the only way to be truly satisfied is to do what you believe is great work.

And the only way to do great work is to love what you do.

If you haven't found it yet, keep looking.

Don't settle.

Steve Jobs
Stanford 2005

Finding Your

Way Forward

Never in history have there been fewer barriers in the way.

No matter where we come from, what our parents did for a living, how much money we have, we all can be unqualified successes.

So who do you want to talk to?
Where do you want to spend your time?
What do you want to learn?

Chris Sacca
University of Minnesota 2011

Achievable goals.

The first step to self-improvement.

J K Rowling
Harvard 2008

You want to put yourself in a place that suits who you are, links you to others . . .

Nobody here knows where the place for you will be. But graduates, we do know there *is* a place for you.

In fact, there are likely many of them. You are going to even create some of those places yourselves, and the world is going to benefit from that.

Atul Gawande
University of North Carolina 2014

You're not going to get very far in life based on what you already know.

You're going to advance in life by what you're going to learn *after* you leave here.

Charlie Munger
University of California Law School 2007

It is my hope that you run out of here, excited, leaning forward, into the wind, ready to take the world by storm. That would be so very fabulous.

My point, I think, is that it is OK if you don't.

You can still wake up one day and find yourself living a life you never even imagined dreaming of . . .

You can wake up one day and find that you are interesting, and powerful and engaged.

Shonda Rhimes
Dartmouth College 2014

If you're not curious, practice being curious. Want to know things. Ask questions.

Anders Holm
University of Wisconsin-Madison 2013

I have a wonderful doctor in LA. Dr Sadeghi. The other day he sent me a picture of an archer. The idea being that when you pull the string of a bow the potential energy is created in the bending of the bow itself. The more the bow is bent, the more potential energy you create.

Failure, challenges, they are just a bending of that bow. The bigger the failure, the more potential energy you have created.

And then you have a choice. What arrow will you dream to be to put in that bow?

Will it be one of resentment, anger, self-loathing, negativity? Or will you dream yourself to be an arrow of opportunity and confidence, and hope and wisdom and generosity?

The choice is yours.

Brad Falchuk

Hobart & William Smith Colleges 2014

127

Enjoy Life. Have fun.

Choose to be happy now: don't wait until you're 'successful', because, honestly, I was as happy when we were unemployed and scrounging around for a buck.

Peter Farrelly
Roger Williams University 2007

In a world where everything is remembered and kept forever, the world you're graduating in to, you should live for the future and the things that you really care about.

Don't live in the past, live in the future.

Eric Schmidt
Carnegie-Mellon University 2009

128

Never underestimate what other people might know.

Sometimes people who seem to be the least possible source of interesting information turn out to be the greatest source imaginable.

David McCullough Jr
Lesley University 2013

You can't change the world alone - you will need some help.

And to truly get from your starting point to your destination takes friends, colleagues, the goodwill of strangers, and a strong coxswain to guide them.

William McRaven
University of Texas 2014

Sometimes, the only way to discover who you are or what life you should lead is to do less planning and more living - to burst the double bubble of comfort and convention and just do stuff. Even if you don't know precisely where it's going to lead - *because* you don't know precisely where it's going to lead.

Daniel Pink
Northwestern University 2014

I believe that there's a lesson in almost everything that you do, and every experience.

And getting the lesson is how you move forward. It's how you enrich your spirit.

And, trust me, I know that inner wisdom is more precious than wealth.

Oprah Winfrey
Stanford 2008

Sometimes the right thing to do will make you feel almost sick to your stomach.

There may come a time you have to SEEK OUT the uncomfortable situation in pursuit of your goal.

Savannah Guthrie
Hobart & William Smith Colleges 2012

Use what money you have to buy experiences, not things.

Don't try to control other people. You can't.

Don't ruminate on bad events.

David Brooks
Sewanee University of the South 2013

(*Careers)* are not a ladder; they're a jungle gym.

As you start your post-HBS career, look for opportunities, look for growth, look for impact, look for mission.

Move sideways, move down, move on, move off. Build your skills, not your resume.

Evaluate what you can do, not the title they're going to give you.

Do real work. Take a sales quota, a line role, an ops job. Don't plan too much, and don't expect a direct climb.

If I had mapped out my career when I was sitting where you are, I would have *missed* my career.

Sheryl Sandberg
Harvard Business School 2012

Do your work.

Drown out your inevitable self-doubt with the work that needs to be done.

Find joy in the process of preparation.

Bradley Whitford
University of Wisconsin 2004

Appearances are often very deceptive, and as Kipling well says, we must:

". . . meet with Triumph and Disaster. And treat those two impostors just the same."

Winston Churchill
Harrow School 1941

I believe we may have reached peak bullshit, and that increasingly those that push back against the noise and nonsense - those who refuse to accept that untruths of politics and commerce, and entertainment and government - will be rewarded.

That we are at the beginning of something important . . .

Go forward with confidence and an eagerness to learn, and to be honest with yourselves and others.

To reject a culture of insincerity by virtue of the example you set in your own lives.

Jon Lovett
Pitzer 2013

Life has a very simple plot.
First you're here, and then you're not.

Eric Idle
Whitman College 2013

We all spend too much time on our iPhones. We track trivia and news, clicking on views and news that all too often confirm what we already believe.

I urge you to carve out time as well for serious books, and sustained thought.

Remember the distinction between information - available anywhere, any time with the touch of a fingertip - and the *knowledge* that comes with mastering a subject and really understanding how things work.

George Stephanopoulos
Franklin & Marshall College 2014

From now on, you had better put yourself in charge of your own education - if you haven't already.

You may have to buck the system.

Don't let the weaknesses of the system become weaknesses of your own.

John Walsh
Wheaton College 2000

You choose how things affect you. You always have that freedom, no matter how much your liberty it curtailed.

You . . . get to choose . . . how things affect you.

Patton Oswalt
Broad Run High School 2008

FINDING YOUR WAY FORWARD

When you take away someone's job, they're devastated because they have equated their life with their job.

Please, please . . . Don't ever, ever have a job. Always, always have a *work*.

John Jacob Scherer
Roanoke College 2010

You don't have to have a dream. I never really had one of these dreams, and so I advocate passionate, dedication to the pursuit of short-term goals.

Be micro-ambitious. Put your head down and work with pride on whatever is in front of you.

You never know where you might end up.

Tim Minchin
University of Western Australia 2013

Not only can you not plan the impact you're going to have, you often won't recognize it. Even while you're having it.

Dick Costolo
University of Michigan 2013

Be wise, because the world needs more wisdom. And if you cannot be wise, pretend to be someone who *is* wise - and then just behave like they would.

Neil Gaiman
University of the Arts 2012

We want to make the strongest case we can for the power of optimism. Even in dire situations, optimism can fuel innovation, and lead to new tools to eliminate suffering.

Bill & Melinda Gates
Stanford 2014

How to Deliver a
Great Speech

**Whether it's Graduation, or any other event,
here are some points on producing
a speech that people will actually
want to listen to**

There are some truly great and insightful graduation speeches that have stood the test of time. They still inspire because they pass on nuggets of hard-earned wisdom, while at the same time being interesting and entertaining. They engage their audience.

The great ones fill your heart with warmth and hope, and connect you to their speaker. They resonate. They inspire. They are the rare ones.

And then there are the others. Most speeches are pretty much instantly forgotten. Usually they fade because they are as exciting as tapioca, and bore their listeners into disconnection. For the true horrors, obscurity is just wishful thinking; the worst of them have attained immortality by redefining tedium.

Top Tips for Speakers

Having spent hundreds of hours listening to and reading thousands of speeches – it's been interesting to be able to form an overview.

It quickly becomes obvious what makes a winner. And what does not.

If you're about to write a graduation speech – or any other speech come to think of it – here are some observations.

If you do take the time to read these, your audience will be endlessly grateful.

1 - *It's really not about you. Honestly, really, truly - no-one out there wants to hear your life story. A graduation day is full of excitable kids and their relieved parents. It's their day. They want to know what it is you have to offer them. What can you say that will help them to lead a better life?*

Top Tips for Speakers

2 - Be generous. Instead of reinforcing how important and successful you have become, give them something important that life has taught you. Something that will really make them reconsider the status quo, and show them how they can enhance their lives.

3 - Share meaningfully. Throughout all your successes, what are the things that are really closest to your heart? What has sustained you? What has the most meaning for you? Why not pass that insight on . . .

4 - It's not a biography lesson. (To reinforce #1 above) Presumably if you've been asked to speak you've had a level of success in some arena - however, the very worst and most boring speeches are the backstory: a chronological list of events and accomplishments. They always end up being ego-ridden and dry, dry, dry. If you want them to listen, keep it interesting. Generally what interests people most - is hearing about them, not you.

5 - *It's not a political rally. If you work in the corridors of power, chances are everyone already knows your stance. Please don't squander this opportunity to add real value to someone's life by reinforcing, or even worse, justifying your own position.*

6 – *Keep it light. You've been invited to talk at a day of celebration. So make your words celebratory. Yes, there may be a lot wrong with the world but this is not the time to dwell on that. Keep focussed on the up-side.*

7 – *Keep it human. The best speakers connect with their audience through the heart. The way to do this is to show them you're human too. Share something that lets them know that.*

8 - *Reframe 'success'. Not all success is quantifiable on the world stage, at the top of the corporate ladder, or within a bank vault. What has your journey through life taught you? Has it changed what 'success' really means to you now?*

Top Tips for Speakers

9 - Don't only talk about success. Not everyone's life will pivot around 'success'. But it's still possible to live a meaningful life. Be inspiring, but not judgmental or confining.

10 – Include Failure. Everyone's life has some. It's the reality of failures and stuff-ups and flaws that make a person interesting, and often more compassionate and nicer to know. Sharing some of yours (even if they're rare) will help you to connect with everyone, and make you much more human and approachable. It will also make you an inspiring example of how you can go on to be a success despite having 'failed' earlier on.

11 – Don't add pressure. There's already enough of that around. Everyone listening to you has the opportunity to 'change the world' but, if that's your focus, frame it as an enticing opportunity. Offer an invitation rather than delivering an obligation. People respond better to enticement than directives.

12 – *Create stories. Bring the important points you want to highlight alive. Tell a (brief) story to make them real. And interesting. And memorable.*

13 – *Make 'em laugh. If you can, it always helps. Nothing makes the human heart warm more than laughter. It doesn't have to be stand-up – wryness and wit work well too. Self-deprecation always hits the mark.*

14 – *Make 'em want more. A good speech is a brief speech. Keeping them interested, laughing and there for only a short time will make you well-liked, well-received and well-remembered. The perfect guest speaker in fact!*

Look Who's Talking

Here are some of the people who have been talking to you. Many names you'll recognise instantly, some maybe not. Either way, they're all included in this book not only because of the success they've achieved, but because they have something to offer you.

Also available:

for more details, and many more quotes:

www.graduationinspiration.com